PLAY BALL WITH A BAND

Roy Agee, *trombone soloist*
The Bob Wilber All-Star Band

To access audio visit:
www.halleonard.com/mylibrary

Enter Code
7651-5906-6540-8115

ISBN 978-1-59615-798-9

EXCLUSIVELY DISTRIBUTED BY

HAL•LEONARD®

Visit Hal Leonard Online at
www.halleonard.com

Contact Us:
Hal Leonard
7777 West Bluemound Road
Milwaukee, WI 53213
Email: info@halleonard.com

In Europe contact:
Hal Leonard Europe Limited
42 Wigmore Street
Marylebone, London, W1U 2RN
Email: info@halleonardeurope.com

In Australia contact:
Hal Leonard Australia Pty. Ltd.
4 Lentara Court
Cheltenham, Victoria, 3192 Australia
Email: info@halleonard.com.au

contents

TROMBONE

WITCHCRAFT

Carolyn Leigh and Cy Coleman
Arranged by Bob Wilber

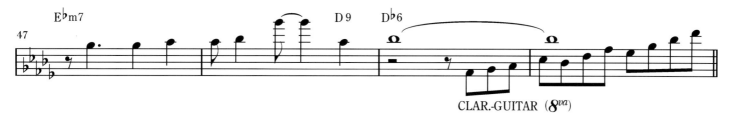

MMO 3972

TROMBONE

ONE FOR MY BABY
(And One More For The Road)

Johnny Mercer and Harold Arlen
Arranged by Bob Wilber

8

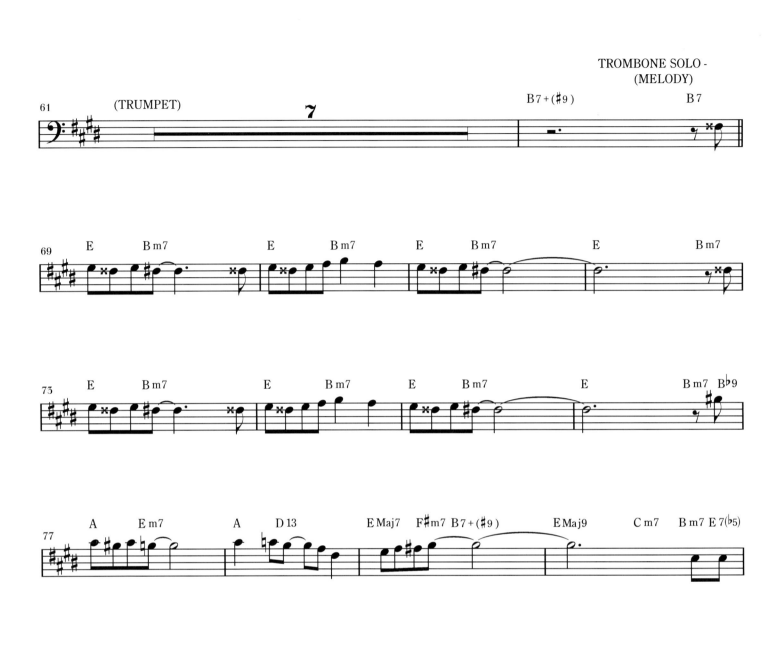

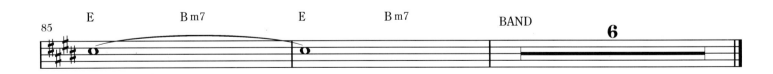

TROMBONE

TENDERLY

Jack Lawrence and Walter Gross
Arranged by Bob Wilber

MMO 3972

TROMBONE

THE CHRISTMAS SONG
(Chestnuts Roasting On An Open Fire)

Mel Torme and Robert Wells
Arranged by Bob Wilber

TROMBONE

AFTER YOU'VE GONE

Henry Creamer and Turner Layton
Arranged by Bob Wilber

TROMBONE

MANHATTAN

Richard Rodgers and Lorenz Hart
Arranged by Bob Wilber

TROMBONE

WHY DON'T YOU DO RIGHT

Joe McCoy
Arranged by Bob Wilber

TROMBONE SOLO
(MELODY)

WHY DON'T YOU DO RIGHT (Get Me Some Money, Too!)
Joe McCoy

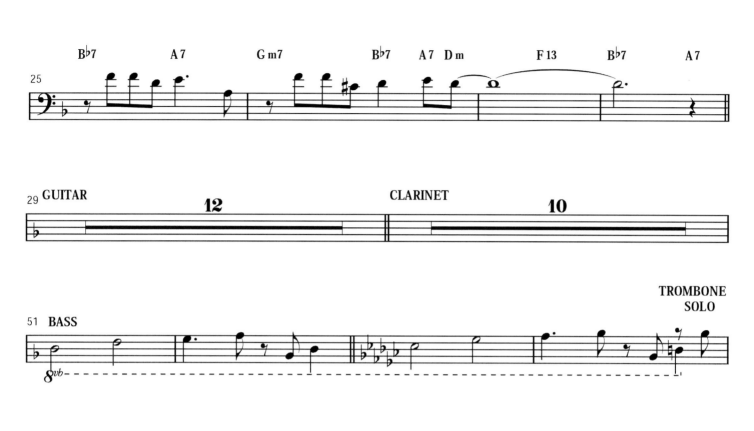

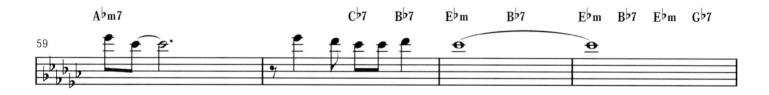

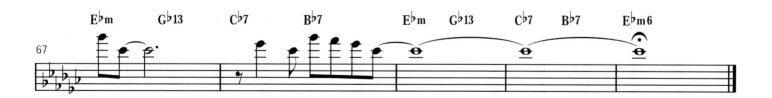

MMO 3972

TROMBONE

I'M GLAD THERE IS YOU

Paul Madeira and Jimmy Dorsey
Arranged by Bob Wilber

I'M GLAD THERE IS YOU(In This World of Ordinary People)
Paul Madeira and Jimmy Dorsey

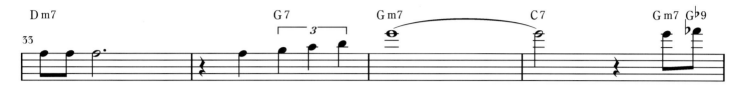

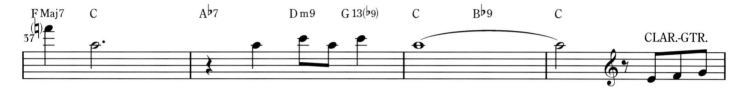

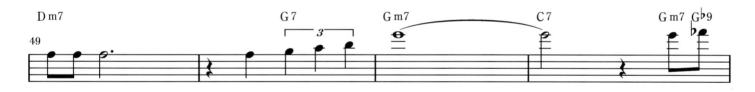

TROMBONE SOLO - (MELODY)

PIANO

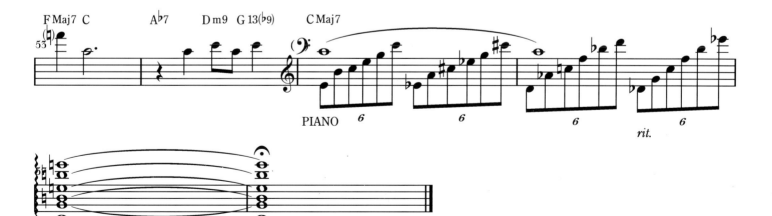

TROMBONE

WHAT A DIFF'RENCE A DAY MADE

Stanley Adams and Maria Grever
Arranged by Bob Wilber

TROMBONE

SENTIMENTAL JOURNEY

Bud Green, Les Brown and Ben Homer
Arranged by Bob Wilber

SENTIMENTAL JOURNEY
Bud Green, Les Brown and Ben Homer
© 1944 (Renewed) MORLEY MUSIC CO. and HOLIDAY PUBLISHING
This arrangement © 2008 MORLEY MUSIC CO. and HOLIDAY PUBLISHING
All Rights Reserved